THROUGH THE STORM

GEORGIA YOUNG-MOORE

Fulton Books, Inc.
Meadville, PA

Published by Fulton Books 2020

ISBN 978-1-64654-690-9 (paperback)
ISBN 978-1-64654-691-6 (digital)

Printed in the United States of America

CONTENTS

I don't think I was ever mad at God; I just

didn't understand the hand I'd been dealt.

You ask me how I know my Redeemer lives.

He kept me alive!

I want to thank the following people:

- To my parents, the late Wade and Maggie Young, for the faith and values instilled in my siblings and me. And for the life lessons they taught by living the example in front of us.
- To my brother, Wade Young, and my sisters, Brenda Young Warren, Linda Young Sanders, Gifberta Young Cook, and Jan Young Morris, for never leaving my side during those trying times. To my nieces and nephews, whom I love dearly.
- To Ki Juana "Kiki" Hopkins and Laverne Jackson, my great friends, who gave me words of encouragement.
- A special thank-you to the late Derresha Shar'Daye Rhinehart, my angel. In the eleven short years that you lived, you brought so much joy into my life. I thank God for the bond we shared. I keep you dear in my heart and think of you every day. I will love you until the end of the earth.
- To the late Derrick Antonio "Dee" Rhinehart, thank you for being a great husband and father and a fantastic provider. Together, we made an angel called Shar'Daye. I will always remember the times we shared and will always keep you in my heart.

- The late James "Boot" and Eliza Rhinehart, for blessing me with Derrick and being great a father- and mother-in-law.
- To the late Pastor Willie Boulware and his lovely wife, Mrs. Barbara Boulware, thank you. Mt. Olive Baptist Church family, you were there for us.
- To the late Pastor Willie Page and his lovely wife, Mrs. Brenda Page, thank you. Friendship Baptist Church Family, you were there for us.
- To Mr. Jim and Gloria Keenon, LaLa Cooper, and the late Hazel Cookson, my guardian angels, thank you.
- To the friends and family that are too many to name individually, thank you.
- To the unmentioned names who are still supporting my family and me, from the bottom of my heart, I genuinely thank you.
- And finally, but certainly not the least, a special thanks to my mighty man of valor, the person whom God released into my life, my husband, Mr. Willie James Moore. I thank God for your love and the support you've shown me while writing this book. You came into my life and helped me restore and rebuild. You brought a joy that I never thought I would experience again. You gave me a family, four children, six grandchildren, and one great-grandchild.

So I want to thank our Sovereign God, who kept me. He caused His face to shine upon me. Not only that, but He also allowed the sun to shine again in my life.

I want to thank Elder Veronica Mayfield for her dedication and talent in helping me write this book.

To God be the glory.

INTRODUCTION

By Elder Veronica Mayfield

B ut I lived.
      My father left me, but I lived.
My mother left me, but I lived.
My only child left me, but I lived.
My husband died and left me, but I lived.
My heart died, but I lived.
My home died, but I lived.
My strength waned, but I lived.
My dreams died, but I lived.
My life died, but I lived.
I lived.
I said, "I lived!
God, why did you leave me here?"
God said, "I need you to live."
"God, but my hope died!"
God said, "You have a purpose. I need you to live."
So, I live…now what?
"But I don't know my purpose, God."
"Just live," He said.
"But how do I live, God?"
"Trust me."
"But I lost everybody…"

"You didn't lose them, Ree. I have them. I need you to keep living. I chose you because you're strong. And I chose you because I know what I put in you. I know you better than you know yourself. I numbered the very hairs on your head. I know how many footsteps I've ordered for you. I've chosen you to be the voice of the silent ones.

"My purpose for you is to help the weary find their way. I've chosen you to lead the brokenhearted back to me. Your tears are not ordinary. They're liquid gold. Your tears will help those who are wounded to get healed. Your breakthrough is their breakthrough. When you cry, demons tremble. The tears you shed are as the rumbling of an earthquake. They soothe anxiety, calm anguish, and relieve pain. Deliverance will manifest because of your shed tears."

"My tears?"

"Yes, your tears. Some people don't know how to release the pressures they're facing. They're too hard-core, and they keep it bottled up inside. Isolated, they are a detriment to themselves, not knowing how close they are to the end. Some eat bullets trying to find relief. Some sit in their garages, in a car filled with exhaust fumes, trying to find relief while others take a handful of God-knows-what kind of pills trying to find relief. Ree, all they need is someone to show them how to pop the top on the place where their tears are stored. Inside, you will find relief."

"Is that all?"

"No, it isn't, but it's a start. Yes, I need you to live. I was there when you wanted to give up. I saw you at your lowest point, and I sent the spirit of life to help you. Sometimes, He's unrecognizable. He came to you on the wings of a dove. He watched over you very carefully and guided your every footstep. From the very first time you called out to me, I was already on the way. While you were yet calling, I was already there. I whispered in your ear, 'Live. You shall be the people's therapy!' Many will be waiting for you. I need you to live."

The Tunnel

The tunnel is not the stopping point. It's the place where you go through the process. In the tunnel is where your water turns into wine. It's where your weaknesses gain strength. In the tunnel is where you find out that "Greater is He in me than he that is in the world!" It is the conduit to bring you out on the other side. The tunnel is an encasement of safety. It protects you from the surrounding waters. People drown in water, but in the tunnel is where God parts your Red Sea.

There is safety in the tunnel.

"Yea, though I walk through the valley of the shadow of death, I will fear no evil." Sound familiar? When you walk through the tunnel, you come out like pure gold. You walk in drab and dreary, but you come out white as snow. Don't fear the tunnel! "I, the Lord, am with you in the tunnel."

Wait a minute! What's that up ahead? Could it be light? Yes, it's light. There is light at the end of the tunnel. "Weeping may endure for a night, but joy cometh in the morning."

"Ree, it is okay to live again. It is okay to love again. It is okay to embrace the change. And don't feel guilty when love calls…Answer it."

It is okay to start over!

—Veronica Mayfield

*****

CHAPTER 1

Faith and Family Values

I magine growing up in the South. It comes with its own unique set of challenges. The foundation for most households was not brick and mortar but faith.

Hello, my name is Georgia Ree Young-Moore. Mostly everyone calls me Ree. I grew up in a small town in Chester, South Carolina. I am the middle child, the fourth of six siblings. Of all my siblings, I was the needy little one. I enjoyed as much alone time as I could get with my parents.

We weren't rich in the typical sense, but our faith and family values were worth millions. We had food, shelter, clothes, and all the love in the world. So by those standards, we were rich. Our family unit was secure. We had a Big Mama, as she was mostly known, who made sure we didn't lack anything. I believe everybody's family has a Big Mama.

Wade and Maggie Young, our parents, were people of faith. They taught us early in life that we must love God. We could depend on God and trust Him. It was no question in our house that everyone was going to Sunday school and Wednesday night Bible study. We often had a prayer breakfast to keep us rooted.

Our family attended the Upper Hope Station Baptist Church in Fairfield County, South Carolina. We went there for years, but years later, after the passing of our father, in 1987, we attended the Friendship Missionary Baptist Church in Chester, South Carolina (my mother's home church).

In April of 1964, on the night I was born, my family moved from the country into the town of Chester, South Carolina. We lived on Columbia Street, and this is where we lived when our parents decided to become foster parents. One of our foster brothers lived with us for ten years until his graduation. My fifth sister Jan was born during the years on Columbia Street. Although she is not my biological sister, my parents picked her up at the hospital when she was only two days old. She was very much loved, and my parents formally adopted her a few years later. In 1975, we moved again on Bird Street in Chester, South Carolina.

Like most typical teenagers, we thought we had the worst parents in the world. While all our peers were out having fun, we were in the church. We had a family gospel group called the Gospel Four. The members were my mother, my younger sister Gifberta, my brother Wade, and I. We traveled all around South Carolina and North Carolina singing songs of praise.

Growing up, I was extremely close to my parents, especially in the kitchen. Watching my parents, I could prepare a full meal for the whole family at the age of ten. If something ever happened to them, I told them I wouldn't make it. Their response to me was "Daughter, the time will come that you will have to rely upon God. Just remember where your help comes from in times of trouble." They went on to remind me that all my help comes from the Lord. Just as they said, I needed to know God for myself and learn how to depend on Him.

In April 1978, my father passed away at the age of forty-six. It was a devastating blow, and I was heartbroken. Many times, I cried out to God. It was in those moments I felt as though I wouldn't make it. But God, in His infinite mercy, gave me the strength to endure.

So now my mother was left alone to raise six children. She became a warrior in prayer. Trials of life tested her faith, but through adversity, she stood firm. She instilled in my brother and sisters that nothing was too hard for God. God was the source of our strength, and He would see us through any situation. In other words, Momma was saying, "On Christ, the solid rock I stand. All other ground is sinking sand."

In May 1988, my mother met and married my stepfather, Herman Brown, and we were blessed to have a second great father in our lives. We called him Mr. Book. My mother and Mr. Book helped raise seven grandchildren, Wanda, Willie,

Alicia, Marques, Dreke, Rock, and Shar'Daye. They called him Gramps. They loved him dearly; he was the only granddad five of them ever knew on this side of the family. Mr. Book passed away in 1994.

Things were okay for a while. Suddenly, my mother started to get ill. My brother, sisters, and grandchildren would alternate, spending the night with my mother. We did this to keep an eye on her during the night.

As we did daily, we all gathered in our mother's apartment. One particular night in November 2001, she convinced us all to go home. We were hesitant to leave, but we honored her request. Little did we know that would be the last time we saw her alive.

Later that night, she called my niece, Alicia, to pick up some items from the store. In the meantime, she was on the telephone talking to her nephew, Alvis. They had so much in common, and she loved talking with Alvis. They would talk for hours about singing and the Lord. It was something they both loved. During the conversation, she stopped talking. After calling her name several times without a response, Alvis hung up and dialed 911. When Alicia returned from the store, she met Alvis trying to get into our mother's apartment. He told Alicia that he called 911, and they were en route. Alicia opened the door and found our mother unresponsive. She administered CPR until the paramedic arrived. Our mother had quietly transitioned.

The anguish and the hurt we felt, words could not express. The glue that held this family together was now gone. We vowed we would keep her legacy alive and take care of each other. The next few months were hard, as we tried to move on without our mother.

Through the storm, *seek him*! He's there guiding you.

CHAPTER 2

Twisted Grief

Four months after the passing of my mother, my only child, my beautiful eleven-year-old, my sweet, smart, energetic, and compassionate baby girl, Shar'Daye, became sick. For three weeks, we went back and forth to the doctors. We were desperately trying to find out what was wrong. Any parent would do whatever's necessary to take care of their children.

Finally, on March 24, my husband and I carried our sweet Shar'Daye to Piedmont Medical Center. Doctors examined her and came to the conclusion that she had a viral infection and wanted to send her home. Shar'Daye never had anything more than a cold; she had never been sick. We insisted on further testing.

After several hours of waiting for the doctor, they finally came back. He advised us that Shar'Daye's white blood cell count was higher than it should be and recommended moving her to the Levine Center at Carolina Medical Center in Charlotte, North Carolina. The next day, the nurse told us the doctor needed to speak with my husband and me. I prepared myself for the worst before speaking with the doctor. I was anxiously pacing back and forth and decided to be brave and take the news standing up.

If memory serves me correctly, I remember hearing the word *leukemia*. I felt the life draining out of me. My legs had no strength to stand. Surely I fainted. The next thing I remember was my husband and one of the doctors picking me up from the floor. It was like being in a bad dream, and I couldn't wake up.

My husband and I wept bitterly as the doctor tried explaining the treatments he foresaw for Shar'Daye. We were hopeful in the doctor's plan of treatment. We asked the doctor to let us tell Shar'Daye, but first, we had to get ourselves together and regain our composure. We prayed for God to give us strength. To help us with the words to say and to help Shar'Daye understand, the nurse gave us a book that would help us explain things to Shar'Daye.

Shar'Daye looked at me bravely and asked, "Mommy, am I going to die?" For a brief moment, time stood still. My heart dropped as I tried to fight back the tears. Finally, I told her, "The doctors here are going to take good care of you. You will never be alone because God is always with you." I stressed to Shar'Daye that her dad and I would be praying. I reminded Shar'Daye to call on the name of Jesus. "If you can't pray, call on His name."

I held a brave face in front of Shar'Daye. Inwardly, my stomach was tied in knots, trying to come to grips with everything the doctor was telling us. How do I process this and keep my sanity? I had two life calamities going on at the same time: grief and sickness. I know I'm not the first to have dealt with it. But I had been stretched about as far as I could.

God, how could this be happening to me? I screamed. I yelled at God. How could this be happening? I just lost my mother. Now, this? My only child—my precious daughter—diagnosed with leukemia. God, I don't understand. Help me understand. Why is this happening? My life had taken a downward spiral.

Shar'Daye needed me. I managed to get myself together and take control. I got focused on getting Shar'Daye well. We settled in after a couple of weeks of treatment. I could almost feel the sun shining in our direction. Things were going okay. I believed God was in the midst of all we were facing. One day during Shar'Daye's treatment, Derrick stepped out of the room briefly. When we were alone, Shar'Daye said to me, "Mommy" you were right. I called on the name of Jesus, and He came and took my hand. I'm not afraid anymore." I was surprised. Shar'Daye had the brightest smile on her face.

She was smiling and saying this at the same time. She'd had an encounter with Jesus. She told me Jesus came and took her by the hand. My heart was overwhelmed. It felt as though it had dropped. Filled with compassion, I asked her to repeat her story. She said, "Mommy, I wasn't afraid when Jesus took me by the hand."

I had to tell someone what Shar-Daye said, but I didn't want to upset Derrick. So later that evening, I called my oldest sister, Brenda, and shared with her what Shar' Daye told me. I needed to get her input on what Shar' Daye said. My sister talked with me and reassured me nothing was going to happen to Shar'Daye. I trusted my family. We promised our mother we would always be there for one another. My brother and sisters helped me stay grounded during this ordeal.

A week after Shar'Daye's encounter, she began having breathing problems. The doctor felt it necessary to put her on oxygen. She was moved to the ICU and watched closely. I was in the waiting room and decided to close my eyes to take a nap. My husband, Derrick, and I didn't get much sleep.

I woke up to the doctor telling my husband that Shar'Daye had stopped breathing. And they were working on her, but Shar'Daye slipped into a coma. *Lord, help me!* I cried. Within the next hours, we talked with so many doctors. After a while, I didn't want to hear anything else from the doctors. I needed to hear from the Lord.

I got out my Bible and began to seek God for strength. I could hear my mother's words—"You're going to have to rely on God for yourself." So I repeated this phrase to myself "It's not over until God says it's over. Whenever God says it's over, then it's over."

One night, I told the nurse that I noticed a difference in Shar'Daye's breathing pattern; I knew this because I used to listen to her and Derrick's breathing when I checked on them nightly at home. She assured me that it was my imagination and nothing had changed. After speaking with the nurse, Michelle, my sister, Linda, convinced Derrick and me to leave and go over to the Marriott (Derrick's part-time job) to get some rest after being at the hospital for twenty-one days. I was hesitating about leaving, especially after noticing her breathing pattern. But after the nurse and my sister told me that, if anything changed, they would call and that I needed to get some rest, I obliged.

A couple of hours after lying down, there was a knock at our room door; it was my sister Linda telling my husband and me that Shar'Daye had passed. Linda was with Shar'Daye when she took her last breath.

On April 15, 2002, everything in my life changed. Shar'Daye went home to be with the Lord. Shar'Daye's passing away broke my heart. My life was changed.

Losing my mother was devastating. Five months later, losing my only child! *God, what are you doing to me? How do I go on? I can't make it!* Admittedly, I knew I would lose my mind. I didn't even know for whom I was grieving. I was locked in this state of mind for months. I needed my mother. I lost my child. *Help me, please. God, help me.*

I must be having a bad dream. I can't seem to wake up from it. Leaving the hospital, we had the longest ride home. Accepting that I could no longer hold my baby girl was unbearable. I had formed a love for her. For nine months, I carried her inside me. I would never again hear her say "Mommy and Daddy, I love you." I would never feel the embrace of her big hugs. I would never again see her big, contagious smile. I felt empty.

My dreams of her graduating from high school and going off to college—I will never have that. And her getting married and having children of her own—I will never see that. They are crushed dreams that will never be possible. Shar'Daye, our pride and joy, was gone. Shar'Daye's passing was as much of a shock to my siblings as it was to Derrick and me.

I knew God would be there for us. But this was a pain like no other. It seemed too hard to bear. I tried to be strong for my husband. We tried all we knew to move on without Shar'Daye. It was very hard. Our lives were changed. Living without Shar'Daye was the hardest thing we ever had to do. Unimaginable!

It is unnatural for a parent to bury a child. My husband and I went to grief counseling for parents that had lost their children. Hearing other parents talk about their child was very familiar to me. They described the hurt, the pain, and the experiences that I knew all too well. But none of them ever shed a tear. I watched it in amazement. It was too quiet—no emotions, no tears, nothing. The hidden feeling seemed strange to me.

When it was our turn to speak about our loss, the first thing I said was "I know for sure our child is with God. I know for sure God has our child wrapped up in His care." Then I began to cry like never before. I tapped into the storage place where God keeps our tears. I cried until that storage place was empty. My husband cried as we consoled each other. Later, I was told I had broken the ice so others could grieve. My tears opened the doorway for the other parents. Now their healing process could begin. Crying is healing and healthy. Not only that, no tears will go to waste; God bottles every single one. I didn't know this at the time, but God was birthing a ministry in me.

It was very hard the following Christmas. Buying a headstone for Shar'Daye's burial plot instead of buying her favorite toys for Christmas was like a Christmas I'd never experienced. It was hard visiting her grave site that Christmas morning. Seeing her picture on the headstone was extremely difficult. My family brought me to Chester County Hospital after this visit.

Through the storm, trust his plans…

CHAPTER 3

Faith in the Storm

I thank God that Derrick and I had a family—friends and church family that loved us and prayed for our strength. In the following years after Shar'Daye's passing, the Mt. Olive Baptist Church in Chester SC held an annual Youth Festival in Shar-Daye's memorial. The neighborhood and hundreds of people attended.

Shar'Daye often talked about becoming a doctor. She was an honor student. I believe she would have become a doctor if she had lived. A couple of years had passed when my husband and I decided to do something to keep Shar'Daye's memory alive. We decided to start a foundation in her honor. We would give scholarships to students who were pursuing a career in healthcare. Education is important. The recipients of the award would have to keep a 3.5 GPA and keep up academically. The idea of funding a scholarship foundation was a great way to give back. However, we had to delay that idea for a while.

My husband, Derrick, was a hard worker. He worked two jobs. His routine on Saturday mornings was cutting our half-acre lawn. He would cut his mother's grass also. Derrick would go to his second job after mowing the lawns. One Saturday afternoon, Derrick became ill going to his second job. So he turned around and went home and got into bed. When I returned home later that afternoon was when I found him lying in bed weak. He was dehydrated. Instead of immediately going to the hospital, he stayed in bed and became weaker. Derrick was very weak by the time I convinced him to let me call an ambulance. The ambulance transported Derrick to Carolinas Medical Center. The doctor admitted him immediately.

The nurses were having trouble getting the IV started. After several attempts, the doctor on duty decided to do a procedure that would place the IV fluids in his neck. Derrick needed flu-ids, and they needed to get an IV started. I was nervous, but I signed the papers for the procedure. They told me it was a simple procedure that would take less than thirty minutes. It took hours. After several hours, I went to the nurse's station and started asking questions. "Where is my husband? Didn't you tell me it would take thirty minutes or less?" Quietly, the nurse stated, "The doctor will come in to talk with you soon." I walked back to the waiting room where my mother-in-law waited patiently.

The doctor came to the waiting room and asked me to come out to discuss Derrick's condition. The doctor told me that during the procedure, Derrick stopped breathing. *What?* They revived him, but he was in critical condition. They moved him to the critical care unit. The only thing I can remember is hearing the doctor say that Derrick had stopped breathing. And the next thing I remember is being picked up off the floor.

After several more hours of waiting, I was allowed to go in to see him. It was devastating to see him hooked up to all those machines. He could not speak, but he knew when I entered his room. He became agitated and tried to remove the breathing tubes.

I never saw my husband like this before. He'd never been sick before except maybe for a cold. His mother told me when he was born that he weighed only one pound. But he quickly grew into a healthy, fine boy. The man in this hospital bed didn't look like my husband. I knew a miracle was needed. I went back to the waiting room to pray and seek God. I prayed, "Lord, I know you don't make mistakes. I know you as a healer. If it's your will, please heal my husband. But if it's not your will, don't let him suffer." Derrick's condition began to decline rapidly. I knew he wouldn't pull through. In my mind, if God took him home, he would be healed; but if he stayed on this side of heaven, we needed a miracle. So again, I prayed for God's will. I know Derrick didn't want to leave me. But I had to be strong for him.

I can imagine Derrick was thinking about things he'd left undone. He was a man who valued his family. Derrick never took anything for granted. He lived a life of servanthood. I have been very blessed to have this caliber of man in my corner. I can imagine he may have been thinking about who will take care of the lawns—*that's my job*. Or perhaps he was thinking about who will make sure Ree is safely home—*that's my job. It's my job to rub her shoulders after a hard day at work. It's my job to take care of the upkeep of our home.* I'm sure he was thinking about the commitment he made to God and me that for better or worse, he would be there. Derrick knew I depended on him. So I can only imagine the conversation he and God were having.

Through the storm, overcome the fear.

CHAPTER 4

Saying Goodbye

All the family gathered together in the waiting room. We were allowed to go in and see him and say our goodbyes. I went over to Derrick and rubbed his forehead. I told him that if he was tired of fighting and wanted to go home and be with the Lord, I would be okay. I loved Derrick; I wanted him to get well, but I didn't want him suffering either. My heart was breaking, but my love for him was more potent than my breaking heart. I told Derrick, "You will be united again with Shar'Daye, and it is okay if you want to be with her." I told him that it would be hard for me, but with the help of the Lord, I would make it. And that I would see him and Shar'Daye again. I kissed his forehead and walked away. As soon as I got to the door of his room, he flatlined. I paused for a second but didn't turn around. I continued walking back to the waiting room. I didn't say a word to any of the family about what just happened. I silently went into a corner and began praying for strength. In less than three years, my entire family unit had gone. My life had fallen apart. In 2005, the world I once knew had become a memory.

How could this be happening to me? My mother, my only child, and now my husband. I cried and prayed, "Lord, I know you've never made a mistake. But I don't know what to do or how I'm going to make it. I need your help!" I went back to an empty house that I once called home. The love of my life was not there anymore. Our child was not here anymore. This place no longer seemed like my home. It was not the bright, happy home to which I'd become accustomed. Home is where the heart is; this I know. But those closest to my heart were gone. I didn't recognize this house; it didn't look the same or feel the same no matter how I changed things around. I was as empty as this house.

Each room of this house overpowered me with memories: family get-togethers, Sunday dinners, birthday parties for Shar'Daye, and my sibling sing-alongs. My anxiety was at another whole level. The pictures of our family—of Derrick, Shar'Daye, and myself. My siblings didn't know what to say to me. They saw my pain up close and personal. I retreated almost back into the infant stage. They cared for me as my mother did. Day and night, my siblings took turns caring for me. It was painful for them to see me this way. They didn't know if I was going to pull through this.

I thank God for my five siblings, Brenda, Linda, Wade, Gifberta, and Jan, who never left my side. I also thank God for Kiki and Laverne and the many other friends and family members who stayed by my side. My sister, Linda, rented her house and moved in with me so I wouldn't have to be in my home alone. My sisters and brother and other family members altered their lives around my mine. They wanted to make sure I would be okay. Whatever they thought I needed, they got it. But they couldn't help me; I needed a miracle. All my days seemed dark and cloudy. I stayed in bed for what seemed like weeks. I needed God's help! I was struggling, and I knew I wasn't going to make it if God didn't intervene. I had more questions than answers. And the only person that could fill in the missing pieces was God. My testament to Derrick is, he was a great husband, father, and provider. I was lost and broken without him. I couldn't think straight. I could no longer be an energetic person, and I didn't want to. My will to go on was gone. All my strength was gone.

My mind went back to when I was younger. My mother told all my siblings and me that a time would come when we would have to rely on God, our help. She said, "The real help comes from the Lord." She told us we needed to know God for ourselves and how to depend on Him—to trust in Him, and He alone will see you through. My mother's words are my reality now. All parents speak into their children's lives if only they would listen. I'm glad I listened. When my mother said, "That time will come," well, it inevitably came for me.

I was in a dark place. I remember putting my hands over my face, and I couldn't see beyond it. I'd never been in a situation that I couldn't see my way out of. But this time, I felt like I couldn't make it. This turn of events had me believing there was no hope or help for me. I had nothing left, and I couldn't see my way. I certainly thought I would lose my mind. I couldn't think straight, and yes, I felt like giving up—like I was hanging from a cliff with only a rope to hold on to, and I was at the end of it. I don't think I was ever mad at God; I didn't understand the hand God dealt me.

Through the storm, remember His promises.

CHAPTER 5

A Present Help

In my darkest moment, I thought about Psalm 46:1 (NKJV), which states, "God is our refuge and strength, a very present help in trouble." I faced my new life, totally trusting in the Word of God. I lived in the power of His might. No doubt God gave me the strength to endure. I replayed my mother's words repeatedly in my mind. The things I said to God in prayer may not have been politically correct, but I poured myself out to God. I came as an empty vessel before a full fountain.

I prayed, "God, I need your help. This is too hard for me, and I can't see my way. Lord, it's just too hard! Lord, I'm leaning and depending on you. You said in your word that you will be with me always and never leave or forsake me [Deut. 6:31b NIV]. God, I need you!" As it was in the days of Jehoshaphat, "God, we know not what to do. But our eyes are on you" (2 Chron. 20:12c). "Right now, God, I don't know what to do, but I'm looking to you. Just let me live and stay in my right mind."

I read Isaiah 41:10 (KJV) daily, which says,

> Fear thou not; for I am with thee, be not dismayed; for I am thy God: I will strengthen thee; yea, I will help thee; yea, I will uphold thee with the right hand of my righteousness.

I still read this scripture daily.

God heard my cry and answered my prayer. When I look down from the cliff and the rope that I was hanging on to, I found more of it. God, who is my lifeline, extended the line. When God lengthens the cord, you have to be willing to accept His extension plan. Sometimes, He will send someone to coddle you, and at other times, He will implement tough love.

God knows what we need and when it's needed. My oldest sister, Brenda, took on the role of a mother. Yes, they gave me what I needed. But to help me survive, God used my siblings in a way I didn't expect. Brenda was adamant about not letting me get too far gone in grief. She wouldn't allow me to get to the point of no return. She told my other siblings, "We have to stop coddling and bring her back to reality."

One day, I told my sister Linda I felt like wallowing on the floor.

And she said, "You will wallow by yourself. We have places to go and things to take care of." Well, as you can imagine, I didn't expect that response. So I got myself together and got in the car with her to take care of business. A single step. Just a single step.

Daily, my burden was a little lighter. During the hardest time in my life, as the poem goes, when you only saw one set of footprints (excerpt from a poem written by Mary Flashback, *Footprints in the Sand*), it was then He carried me. We do not realize when God is holding us. I have no other explanation except God brought me through. When you get on the other side of the storm and look back, there's no denying the power of God. Looking back, I noticed all the dark and gloomy days. However, looking forward, the sun began to shine again. Of course, it was always there, but the pain of it all had me blind. Then I wanted to get out of bed, and I started to think clearer.

I thank God. He came to my rescue. He made what I thought was an impossible situation possible. What's impossible to man is just right with God (Luke 18:27 KJV). The possibilities of God are limitless. The only reason I'm alive and in my right mind is because of the help of the Lord.

We can triumph over any struggles we face with God's help. There is nothing too hard for God (Jer. 32:17 AMP). Whatever the situation, remember, with God, all things are possible if you believe (Mark 9:23 KJV).

At some point or another, you might be overwhelmed with trials. And like others, you feel like your problem is impossible to bear and you can't make it. But with God's help, we can make it. He can make it possible. Luke 1:37 says, "For nothing will be impossible with God." After the deaths of my family, I was counted out by many. Some said I would never make it. I thought that as well. But every time that thought came in my mind, God quickly changed my thought pattern. He filled my mind with His promises like Jeremiah 29:11, which says, "For I know the plans I have you for declares the Lord, plans to prosper you and not harm you, plans to give you a future and a hope."

Losing a loved one is hard. And I wasn't prepared for losing a loved one. We know that this earth is not our home. We fail to realize the only way to get to heaven is through the portal of death. Quite honestly, losing a child is one of the hardest experiences any parent will ever face. To me, a child dying before the parent is unnatural. But as I previously stated, nothing is too hard for God. So please know, if you're reading this, God brought me through, and He will bring you through as well.

I received many letters and cards of encouragement during that time in my life. One note in particular stayed with me. It came from a lady who would help anyone and everyone. She, too, lost her first husband and child and thought the same as I did, that her life was over. She wanted to encourage me and let me know that the sun would shine again; that God would see me through. Lastly, she said, "God will use my life to be a testimony for many." God has a way of turning things around. God will provide for those who grieve, and He will give you beauty for ashes, the oil of gladness instead of mourning, and a garment of praise instead of a spirit of despair (Isa. 61:3 NIV).

Through the storm, mercy endures forever.

CHAPTER 6

A Faithful God

The journey will be uncomfortable, but God will give you the strength to endure. I am speaking from personal experience. God will empower you with the strength to cope every day. I am grateful that God's mercies will never run out; daily, He renews them. No matter how dark your situation may be or how hard your problem may seem, God is faithful. There is nothing too big for Him to handle. I know it may sound like a canned response to grief, but it's not. Redirect your sights. If a deer changes position in the woods, you redirect your view. Don't continue to look where he was. Look to where he went. Change the focus of your right-now. And look to the hills from whence cometh your help. Listen, the Lord is close to the brokenhearted and saves the crushed in spirit (Ps. 34:18 KJV). If you take a step in His direction, you activate a promise. Yes, it is just that easy. I didn't say you would immediately feel better, but the journey of a thousand miles begins with the first step (Lao Tzu, Chinese proverb).

Still, cry if you have to and scream if you must, but do it moving forward. Eventually, your emotions will move from sadness to serenity and from tranquility to a state of freedom from the storm. Continue to climb your way to the top. How? Get involved. A man who does nothing gets nothing. As you shift from one emotion to the other, don't feel guilty for beginning to feel better. Change is called progress. Trust the process. Right now, wherever you are, say it out loud, "God, I'm trusting your process!"

Also remember, God is actively involved in our suffering. You can feel His presence. He'll be there for you. Take your eyes off your situation and place them on God. God will never leave you. He is our refuge and strength, a very present help in times of trouble (Ps. 46:1 KJV). God promised we would not allow temptation beyond what we can bear (1 Cor. 10:13 KJV). He vowed to stand by us in our pain, to walk with us through the valley of the shadow of death (Ps. 23:4; Isa. 43:2). A faithful God, His love for us is incomparable. He's committed to sustain and keep us, to carry you through trials great and small.

I was blessed to have godly parents who taught me the love of Christ and a Heavenly Father who cares for me and instructs me to cast all my cares on Him (1 Pet. 5:7 KJV).

Finally, please do not forget, the Lord our God shares your pain. I am a living testimony. Without Him, I wouldn't be here today. And I certainly wouldn't be in my right mind. I pray you've been encouraged through my experiences. I pray the challenges I faced will empower you to live on in the face of adversity. Is it smooth sailing? No way. But is it doable? Yes, it is. Just as God brought me through this challenging journey, He will bring you through as well. Trust!

CHAPTER 7

Restoration

It's been five years now, and partially, I'm adjusted to my new normal. Frankly, my entire family was affected by the circumstances of my life. We took family vacations together. On one occasion, my brother Wade loaded us all in a van, and we just went sightseeing up the eastern seaboard. All points north visiting family and sightseeing. It was refreshing for all of us.

I finally went back to work; nothing too exciting was happening. Wade would give me advice as a father would give to a daughter. He told me things like "Be careful out there. If you ever start dating again, you have to be careful of some men." He told me the typical things like a father would. Wade and my sisters were my dates, and I was the third wheel. We went to the movies and had dinner as a family. They were all very protective, especially Wade.

As fate would have it, a young man came in to take care of his business at my place of employment. He was a widower as well. We exchanged pleasantries—the "good to see you" kind of conversation and the "'I hope you're doing well" sort of talk. I was genuinely happy to see him thriving after the loss of his spouse. We talked and laughed because we had so much in common. His wife passed in October 2006, and my husband passed in October 2005. In one of our many conversations, he said to me, "I think you need to let me take you out to dinner." And the rest, as they say, is history. God restored my life.

Today, I have a new husband, Willie James Moore, and a new family. His children are our children; Willie has three daughters, one son, six grandchildren, and one greatgrandchild. To God be all the glory! God did not leave me in the shape that I was in; the Potter put me back together again. Restoration feels mighty good. I am blessed and divinely favored.

Don't let anyone put stipulations on your life. Don't let anyone tell you it's too early to think about starting over. No one has the right to make you feel guilty for living again. Don't let grief leave you in the valley of despair. In Ezekiel 37, God asks the question, "Can these bones live?" What's your answer?

The End

Dedicated in loving memory of the late Derrick Antonio Rhinehart and Derresha Shar'Dye Rhinehart

The Derresha Shar'Daye Rhinehart Scholarship Foundation (DSR) was founded in 2008 by Georgia Young-Moore in memory of her only child, Derresha Shar'Daye Rhinehart, who passed away in 2002 shortly after being diagnosed with leukemia. The organization obtained its 501 (c)(3) status in 2009.

DSR Center of Hope Members

The mission of the DSR Center of Hope is to inspire hope by providing programs that strengthen, empower, and improve the community.

ABOUT THE AUTHOR

Georgia's story began with faith and the family values that her beloved parents instilled in her and her five siblings at an early age, followed by numerous grief experiences she experienced after losing her parents, her only child, and her husband. Georgia is compassionate about bringing hope, encouragement, and comfort to those who are in need. Through these life experiences, Georgia's compassion to help others led her to start the DSR Center of Hope, a nonprofit organization she started in memory of her daughter, Derresha Shar'Daye Rhinehart, in 2008; and under the nonprofit umbrella, she also founded the Circle of Parents Experiencing Grief Support Group (COPEG). The support group is free of charge and is open to any parent who has experienced the death of a child. All races and nationalities are welcome to call 803-448-6870 or to visit their website, dsrcenterofhope.com.

CPSIA information can be obtained
at www.ICGtesting.com
Printed in the USA
JSHW041504071120
9395JS00001B/32